THE DIFFERENT STAGES OF Deliverance

Apostle Patricia L. Tard
Copyright ©2022 Apostle Patricia L. Tard

THE DIFFERENT STAGES OF Deliverance

Apostle Patricia L. Tard

Copyright ©2022 Apostle Patricia L. Tard

The Different Stages of Deliverance
Deliverance Manual
Copyright ©2022 Apostle Patricia L. Tard
Published by Never A-Mis Enterprises, LLC
P.O. Box 2298
Byron, GA 31008-2298
www.neveramisenterprises.com

ISBN: 9798985059748

Printed in the United States of America

All rights reserved.
No part of this publication may be reproduced, stored in a retrieval system, or transmitted in any form or by any means - for example, electronic, photocopy, recording - without the prior written permission of the publisher. The only exception is brief quotations in printed reviews. The authorized purchaser has been granted a nontransferable,

nonexclusive, and noncommercial right to access and view this electronic publication, and purchaser agrees to do so only in accordance with the terms of use under which it was purchased or transmitted. Participation in or encouragement of piracy of copyrighted materials in violation of author's and publisher's right is prohibited.

KJV – *KingJames Version* Scripture taken from the King James Version. Authorized *KingJames Version – Public Domain*

AMP -*Amplified Version* Scripture copyright ©2015 by The Lockman Foundation, La Habra, CA 90631. All rights reserved.

Merriam-Webster Online Dictionary copyright ©2021 by Merriam-Webster, Incorporated

All contents of the Services are © Merriam-Webster, Incorporated or its licensors. All rights reserved. Merriam-Webster Online (www.Merriam-Webster.com) is copyrighted ©2021 by Merriam-Webster, Incorporated.

Table of Contents

Introduction

Chapter One – Salvation.

Chapter Two – Bondage.

Chapter Three – Repentance of sins.

Chapter Four – Behavior issues.

Conclusion

About The Author

INTRODUCTION

This book consists of my lessons of deliverance I experienced in my life. Through years of suffering, being physically abused; and severely abused mentally, God sustained me. He kept me in the midst of pain and hurts, and throughout abandonment. Because I went through the process and allowed God to heal, deliver and make me free, I am used by Him to help others become free of demonic strongholds … the spirit of divination; the spirit of jealousy; the lying spirit; the perverse spirit; the spirit of haughtiness; the spirit of heaviness; the spirit of whoredom; the spirit of infirmity; the deaf and dumb spirit; spirit of bondage; the spirit of fear; the seducing spirit; the spirit of the anti-christ; the spirit of error; the poverty spirit, and the spirit of death. Demonic oppressions hold people in bondage. God has given me the wisdom, knowledge, and Authority to help train an Army of Warriors to administer true deliverance to those in need.

Since 1984, I have had multiple opportunities of OJT (Onsite/On the Job Training) throughout different deliverance/Apostolic ministries. In OJT (Onsite/On the Job Training), I assisted individuals in deliverance in a one – on – one setting, as well as with five-fold ministry leaders in their services. I have seen the Power of God show up and move on behalf of the people in need. My personal experience has aided me to be able to recognize the different patterns and stages of deliverance; but it is The Holy Spirit Who grants revelation knowledge to do the work.

Deliverance is a Very broad area, and it has numerous facets. The churches either do not know how or are not teaching deliverance the way God wants it to be taught. You have to experience it and LIVE

IT… Instead, it has turned into a money game. Spiritual warfare is REAL! In order to be effective, you have to have been through it and STILL living a Holy life unto Jesus. I often tell people, "If this is not your expertise, stay in your lane!"

There are diverse types of deliverance, and there are different processes to obtain deliverance. Deliverance refers to the act of cleaning a person of demons and evil spirits to address the problems that have manifested in their lives. The various stages of deliverance are important because we are a three-part trichotomy, body, soul, and spirit.

The root cause of why these said entities have entered in and have the authority to oppress the person need to be addressed. When administering deliverance, one MUST make sure their life is clean! This means your "house" must be in order and free from having skeletons in your closet. The demonic forces WILL expose and call you out, quickly if there is anything there.

I have experienced tremendous warfare, hits, attacks, and demons in clusters while helping others get delivered. I have seen things that have had me shaking in my boots. Diverse levels … different devils.

Even with ALL of the things I have seen and experienced, I had to be strong in the Lord and not fear; and most Definitely filled with Holy Ghost power! In this hour, with the world coming off of the heels of a global pandemic, deliverance is ***VERY MUCH NEEDED!!***

Chapter One

Salvation.

The first stage or step of deliverance is salvation. You can be saved but not delivered. According to Merriam Webster Dictionary, salvation is the deliverance from the power and effects of sin. Being made free comes from the truth of the Word of God. **John 6:63KJV**, *"It is the spirit that quickeneth; the flesh profiteth nothing: the words that I speak unto you, they are spirit, and they are life."*

Theologically, it is the deliverance from sin and consequences; believed by Christians through faith in Christ Jesus, and their relationship with Him. Just because you are saved as a Christian does not mean you do not need or have been delivered. If you want deliverance, it is in the Word of God. There is a process, a method to the madness! In **Psalms 51:5*AMP*,** David said, *"I was brought forth in [a state of] wickedness; In sin my mother conceived me [and from my beginning I, too, was sinful]."* We do not fall into sin, the majority of them are premeditated through disobedience; then we act it out. Once is conceived, we then have to go through deliverance to be made free, which brings redemption, deliverance, saving, help, or reclamation (the act of reclaiming or a state of being); restoration or restoring. These are the stages of the process that brings back its original state.

God is trying to get us back to the place where Adam and Eve knew no sin; this leads you to salvation through repentance. When John the Baptist came on the scene, he was declaring, "Repent! The Kingdom of Heaven is at hand!" Jesus was in the same vein when He began His ministry preaching the same thing … "Repent for the Kingdom of God is at hand. Kingdom is Power!" Jesus came to set us free!

We must ask ourselves what was the purpose of Jesus coming? I am talking about stages of deliverance. We are saved through the shred blood of Jesus Christ and His finished work on the cross; however, the soul that keeps willfully sinning shall surely die! **Roman 5:9***AMP*, *"Therefore, since we have now been justified [declared free of the guilt of sin] by His blood, [how much more certain is it that] we will be saved from the [b]wrath of God through Him."* Also, **Romans 10:9-10***AMP*, *"because if you acknowledge and confess with your mouth that Jesus is Lord [recognizing His power,* *authority, and majesty as God], and believe in your heart that God raised Him from the dead, you will be saved. ^{10} For with the heart a person believes [in Christ as Savior] resulting in his justification [that is, being made righteous—being freed of the guilt of sin and made acceptable to God]; and with the mouth he acknowledges and confesses [his faith openly], resulting in and confirming [his] salvation."*

Furthermore, **Hebrews 9:27-28*AMP***, *"And just as it is appointed and destined for all men to die once and after this [comes certain] judgment, ^{28} so Christ, having been* *offered once and once for all to bear [as a burden]* [a] *the sins of many, will appear a second time [when he returns to earth], not to deal with sin, but to bring salvation to those who are eagerly and confidently waiting for Him."*

Death and judgment are inevitable. From the beginning, we were lost and on our way to hell, so we needed to be saved. The only thing required of us is to believe, obey, and have faith in Jesus Christ. It is the works of the flesh that bind us up and keep us in sin. It is cause and effect.

HALLELUJAH!! The mandate is to cast

out anything that is not like Jesus Christ, in Jesus Name!

It was a process and stages of deliverance that took place to get to us where we are now as born-again believers. **Romans 5:12KJV**, *"Therefore, just as sin came into the world through one man, and death through sin, so death spread to all people [no one being able to stop it or escape its power], because they all sinned."* In the same instance, another man which was Jesus Christ by His Sacrificial Death, paid for our Redemption.

The stages of Deliverance in Christian theology is the study of God's redemption. In the Greek, it is apolytrosis, the deliverance of Christians from sin. In the New Testament, "redemption" refers to both deliverance from sin and freedom from captivity. Salvation includes Deliverance from Evil; Both are temporary. **2 Corinthians 4:18***AMP*, *"So we look not at the things which are seen, but at the things which are unseen; for the things which are visible are temporal [just brief and fleeting], but the things which are invisible are everlasting and imperishable."* In other words, what we see now is temporary, but what we do not see is more real than this world, which are Spiritual!

The word tells us that we must worship Him in Spirit and in Truth. **John 4:23-24***AMP*, *"But a time is coming and is already here when the true worshipers will worship the Father in spirit [from the heart, the inner self] and in truth; for the Father seeks such people to be His worshipers. God is spirit [the Source of life, yet invisible to mankind], and those who worship Him must worship in spirit and truth."* Once we have true deliverance, we can now worship in Spirit and in Truth because all temporal things have been removed from us and we have gone back to original place of no sin.

We still need to be mindful so as to not become entangled in fleshy works that could allow for us to be in bondage again. I do believe we can fall out of fellowship and relationship with God which leads us into a backslidden state of mind. If one does fall into a backslidden state, going through the deliverance process will be necessary.

I drafted this book to set the captives free. While in my bed years ago the Holy Spirit give me **Isaiah 61:1-3*AMP***, *"The*

Spirit of the Lord God is upon me, Because the Lord has anointed and commissioned me To bring good news to the humble and afflicted; He has sent me to bind up [the wounds of] the brokenhearted, To proclaim release [from confinement and condemnation] to the [physical and spiritual] captives And freedom to prisoners, To proclaim [a] the favorable year of the Lord, [b] And the day of vengeance and retribution of our God, To comfort all who mourn,

To grant to those who mourn in Zion the following: To give them a [c]turban instead of dust [on their heads, a sign of mourning],

The oil of joy instead of mourning,

The garment [expressive] of praise instead of a disheartened spirit.

So they will be called the trees of righteousness [strong and magnificent, distinguished for integrity, justice, and right standing with God],

The planting of the Lord, that He may be glorified.

He called my name and said, "I want you to set the Captives Free! I sat straight up in my bed and said, "I don't want to set the captive free!" I was yelling like a mad woman because He called my name three times. The call got to me! I did not know this was the Gospel the Good News of Salvation. The Good News is preaching the death, burial, and resurrection of Jesus Christ for the saving of souls. It is about the lost souls! Glory to God!!!! Just think back to when I talked about John the Baptist and Jesus saying, "Repent! The Kingdom of God is at hand. The purpose of Jesus Christ coming was to redeem us back The Father. That was the entire plan.

Allow me to show you something …
We are saved and being saved all the time.
Hosea 4:6*AMP*, *"My people are destroyed for lack of knowledge [of My law, where I reveal My will]. Because you [the priestly nation] have rejected knowledge, I will also reject you from being My priest. Since you have forgotten the law of your God, I will also forget your children."* A significant amount of us cannot get this or receive due to not changing our mindset and thought process!

While I was writing, the Spirit spoke, "Speak Truth to Power." My God,

GLORY!! We have to strive for perfection; righteous living and live all we know how. It is about the principles which people cannot argue. Salvation is the saving of the soul from sin and its consequences. We are made of spirit, soul and body which is the flesh, when we are born again your Spirit belongs to God. The soul consists of our mind, will, emotions, intellect, and imagination. The mind is the battle ground where we make decisions in our lifestyle. Some decisions are good, and some are not! The enemy always fights us in your mind. The enemy is fighting many of you right now reading this book. Sin is not an issue with God, our sins are not being imputed to us. **2 Corinthian 5:21***AMP* *"He made Christ who knew no sin to [judicially] be sin on our behalf, so that in Him we would become the righteousness of God [that is, we would be made acceptable to Him and placed in a right relationship with Him by His gracious lovingkindness]."* Sin was charged to Jesus Christ's account. He already paid for our sins, past, present, and future. Without the shedding of the Blood of Jesus Christ, there would be no remissions of our sins. Our spirit got saved, but our flesh did not! Living in this human flesh, the spirit and the flesh will always war against one another. Glory to God!!!

Chapter Two

Bondage.

Everyone inherits various chains of bondage due to Adam and Eve's choice to seek wisdom apart from Gods' provision. Deliverance cannot be fully obtained solely by salvation. Being freed from bondage is a process; yet we need to die to our flesh daily. Not only do we have to die to our flesh daily, but we have to put work to mature/perfect our life resulting from receiving salvation. Paul is said in **Philippians 2:12***AMP*, *"So then, my dear ones, just as you have always obeyed [my instructions with enthusiasm], not only in my presence, but now much more in my* *absence, continue to work out your salvation [that is, cultivate it, bring it to full effect, actively pursue spiritual maturity] with awe-inspired fear and trembling [using serious caution and critical self-evaluation to avoid anything that might offend God or discredit the name of Christ].*" Salvation is a gift from God, we cannot work for it. **Philippians 2:12 KJV** says, *"work out your own soul salvation with fear and trembling."* Paul understood the challenges a new believer would experience. The convert's lifestyle cannot be changed with their own efforts. There are who leaders preach the "grace" message the wrong way it misrepresents the truth and gives us a license to sin. This is why people keep falling into sin due to leaders not teaching sound doctrine in righteous and Holy living. Anything goes these days, and a lot of leaders' co-sign sin and wonder why deliverance is needed. **Romans 7:14-15***AMP*, *"We know that the Law is spiritual, but I am a creature of the flesh [worldly, self-reliant—carnal and unspiritual], sold into slavery to sin [and serving under its control]. For I do not understand my own actions [I am baffled and bewildered by them]. I do not practice* *what I want to do, but I am doing the very thing I hate [and yielding to my human nature, my worldliness—my sinful capacity].*

The Bible tells us to lay hands on no man suddenly, spirits do transfer whether we believe it or not. We must find out what bondages are present and how the devil is operating through them. Discovering the bondages the devil has authority over, gives us information of how to help prepare them for deliverance. There are times, we want to lay hands and prophesy and pray for people, yet we do not have a clue of what spirit by which they are bound. **1 Timothy**

5:22**AMP***, "Do not hurry to lay hands on anyone [ordaining and approving someone for ministry or an office in the church, or in reinstating expelled offenders], and thereby share in the sins of others; keep yourself free from sin."* We should not be so quick in laying hands on everybody. Whatever spirits they are dealing with, we are opening ourselves up to receive them. Keep yourself pure! Make sure your spirit is clean.

If you lay your hands on a person and your spirit is not right those demons will expose you! You cannot play with any demons. I have experienced more than my share of demons in my lifetime. I tell them, "Look you better take those demons with you and get out of here in the Name of Jesus." I do not entertain any demons. I cast them out!! Most spirits are deeply rooted. Those that are deeply rooted will require greater warfare to remove. They must be cast out in the Name of Jesus! This is war! The Holy Spirit plays the most vital role in this step of the process for deliverance (Holy Spirit Is/should be present throughout the deliverance process!). I must point out everything is not a demon. Sometimes people just act a fool. We are quick to declare a demon, when in reality it is something else. Most of the time it is us! A lot of us are mean as hell; not happy and want everybody else to be miserable with them. There are certain stages we need deliverance that must be recognized. Discernment, wisdom, and knowledge assist us to confront the various issues in deliverance.

Chapter Three

Repentance of sins.

The next stage or step of deliverance is repentance of sins; this begins and brings about deliverance through confessions of said sins; confessing any illegal grounds which has opened doors for the enemy. Not only does it expose how the enemy gained access, but confession also removes strongholds; ungodly soul ties; vows; word curses; and breaks generational curses passed through the blood line. Generational curses are connected through your mama and daddy's DNA. We must bind and cast out those spirits. The word of God tells us in **Mark 3:27KJV**, *"But no one can go into* *a strong man's house and steal his property unless he first overpowers and ties up the strong man, and then he will ransack and rob his house."* This is why Jesus came to plunder (the devils' goods, which are the souls of men). **John 17:15*KJV*,** *"I do not ask You to take them out of the world, but that You keep them and protect them from the evil one."* **Luke 4:18*KJV*,** *"The Spirit of the Lord is upon Me (the Messiah), Because He has anointed Me to preach the good news to the poor. He has sent Me to announce release (pardon, forgiveness) to the captives, And recovery of sight to the* *blind, To set free those who are oppressed (downtrodden, bruised, crushed by tragedy)."* **Luke 11:25-26*AMP*,** *"And when it comes, it finds the place swept and put in order. Then it goes and brings seven other spirits more evil than itself, and they go in [the person] and live there; and the last state of that person becomes worse than the first."* When we go back and forth through those doors; in and out of sin, you gain more demons. It is important we repent privately and/or openly before God exposes us openly. We cannot give up. We must come clean.

Chapter Four

Behavior issues.

The next stage or step of deliverance is dealing with behavioral issues. Some of these are nothing but what society and medical professionals are calling mental illnesses. Everything is not mental illness; it is bondage of the devil caused by deeply rooted sin. If you have Holy Ghost Power within, cast that spirit out in the Name of Jesus; then there will be no mental illness. Jesus cast out demon spirits, which was most of His ministry. We have quite a few in the Body of Christ who are not equipped to cast demons out. They play with the demons, and this keeps the people in bondage. A large majority in the Body of Christ do not believe in demon spirits. Unfortunately, a lot of them are bound themselves. Look at the Church today … No Power … No Glory! **1 Samuel 4: 21-22*AMP*,** *"And she named the boy [b]Ichabod, saying, "The glory has left Israel," because the ark of God had been taken and because of [the deaths of] her father-in-law and her husband. She said, "The glory has left Israel, for the ark of God has been taken."* God has given us power and authority to cast out demons in Jesus' name. Quite a few churches do not know how to conduct deliverance services. Most deep-rooted issues are more severe than others.

Unforgiveness is the root cause of cancer and other related diseases (resentment, bitterness, tormenting spirits). **Mark 11:25-26***AMP*, *"Whenever you [a]stand praying, if you have anything against anyone, forgive him [drop the issue, let it go], so that your Father who is in heaven will also forgive you your transgressions and wrongdoings [against Him and others]. [b][But if you do not forgive, neither will your Father in heaven* *forgive your transgressions."* Yet, we will not forgive others! How can you hold people hostage when God has instructed us to forgive them? There are conditions to this word of instruction. We can pray all we want as they bounce off the wall. We are always trying to justify with excuses, "You don't know what they did to me!" Yes, it was bad, ugly, and cruel; but who are you to hold them hostage if God has said to forgive them! I cannot stress this obedience enough.

There are other behavioral issues many need deliverance from. Self-Un-forgiveness keeps a stronghold in our lives. We must forgive ourselves. Forgiving ourselves is just as important as forgiving others. Holding onto guilt is a pity pot in our heart and mind and keeps depression operating. Self-hatred; low self-esteem; and low self-worth of who God said you open doors for diseases in the body; lupus is one of them. Rejection is based on a false identity or a false image of who we thought we were. A common thought often used among the rejected is, "Nobody loves me. They do not like me." You have to love yourself first!

False guilt/false fear comes from always thinking something is going to happen and peaking negative things. If we continue to do this, it starts to become people pleasing. **Proverbs 18:21***AMP*, *"Death and life are in the power of the tongue, And those who love it and indulge it will eat its fruit and bear the consequences of their words."*

When we are blaming ourselves for everything that is wrong and could go wrong, we cannot distinguish false guilt from true guilt, which leads to double mindedness. **James 1:8***AMP*, *"A double-minded man, unstable and restless in all his* *ways [in everything he thinks, feels, or decides]."* Strongholds of wrong thinking patterns begin to set up in the mind. Next, once have accepted fear/becoming fearful, the fear cripples us.

When a person has experienced trauma in their life, we must be lead them to a place of emotional healing. This is the Holy Spirits job. He will not force anyone or go to a place no one is not willing to allow Him access. The Holy Spirit will not force our will, nor dwell in a place He is not welcomed. The Holy Spirit is a gentleman.

They must understand and come to a place where they know God loves them and He wants them whole. The only way demons can be removed is recognizing where they gained access and close it by going through the deliverance process. Repentance through praise and worship is a wonderful place to begin. Renunciation and confessing Scriptures of deliverance and breaking of curses and covenants made aloud that will give awareness of what God is doing for you. **Psalms 91***AMP*, *"He who dwells in the shelter of the Most High Will remain secure and rest in the shadow of the*

Almighty [whose power no enemy can withstand].

I will say of the Lord, "He is my refuge and my fortress, My God, in whom I trust [with great confidence, and on whom I rely]!" For He will save you from the trap of the fowler, And from the deadly pestilence. He will cover you and completely protect you with His pinions, And under His wings you will find refuge; His faithfulness is a shield and a wall. You will not be afraid of the terror of night, Nor of the arrow that flies by day, Nor of the pestilence that stalks in darkness, Nor of the destruction (sudden death) that lays waste at noon. A thousand may fall at your side And ten thousand at your right hand, But danger will not come near you. You will only [be a spectator as you] look on with your eyes And witness the [divine] repayment of the wicked [as you watch safely from the shelter of the Mos High]. Because you have made the Lord, [who is] my refuge, Even the Most High, your dwelling place, No evil will befall you, Nor will any plague come near your tent. For He will command His angels in regard to you, To protect and defend and guard you in all your *ways [of obedience and service]. They will lift you up in their hands, So that you do not [even] strike your foot against a stone. You will tread upon the lion and cobra; The young lion and the serpent you will trample underfoot. Because he set his love on Me, therefore I will save him; I will set him [securely] on high, because he knows My name [he confidently trusts and relies on Me, knowing I will never abandon him, no, never]. He will call upon Me, and I will answer him; I will be with him in trouble; I will rescue him and honor him. With a long life I will satisfy him And I will let him see My salvation."*

CONCLUSION

Extending forgiveness speaks about our character and our willingness to be free and whole. **Mark 11:24-26***AMP*, *"For this reason I am telling you, whatever things you ask for in prayer [in accordance with God's will], believe [with confident trust] that you have received them, and they will be given to you. Whenever you stand praying, if you have anything against anyone, forgive him [drop the issue, let it go], so that your Father who is in heaven will also forgive you your transgressions and wrongdoings [against Him and others]. [But if you do not forgive,* *neither will your Father in heaven forgive your transgressions."*

Forgiveness coupled with renewing our minds will place us on the road to deliverance and healing. **Romans 12:2AMP**, *"And do not be conformed to this world [any longer with its superficial values and customs],*
ye [a]transformed and progressively changed [as you mature spiritually] by the renewing of your mind [focusing on godly values and ethical attitudes], so that you may prove [for yourselves] what the will of God is, that which is good and acceptable

and perfect [in His plan and purpose for you]."

The bottom line is demons **MUST** be cast out; all spirits **MUST** be removed before total victory is assured in Jesus Name. The Final Stage or step of Deliverance is to bring the people back to wholeness. Once they are delivered, they have the opportunity to pursue God. Deliverance is a process! Please remember, deliverance is not a onetime event; it is an ***ongoing process***!

CLOSING PRAYER

FATHER GOD IN THE NAME OF JESUS I HAVE GIVEN THESE YOUR PEOPLE WHAT YOU HAVE GIVEN ME TO SAY. I PRAY YOU WILL CONTINUE TO SAVE SET

FREE HEAL AND DELIVER IN JESUS NAME. WE THANK YOU FATHER GOD FOR WHAT YOU HAVE DONE AND WHAT YOU ARE DOING AND ALREADY DONE NOW IN JESUS NAME. AMEN.

About The Author

Apostle Patricia L. Tard

Apostle Tard has been in ministry for over 38 years. She is the founder of Women of Wisdom Ministry, Inc. Over the years, Apostle Tard has personally worked and trained other Apostles, Prophet and Pastors called into the deliverance ministry. She states, "It is important to understand how to conduct and be effective in a deliverance service. People want their Freedom and Liberty. Where the Spirit of the Lord is there is liberty!!!"

Apostle Patricia L. Tard is available for to teach and minister deliverance and train leaders and their ministry staff in deliverance.

Contact Information

Email
Patriciat981@gmail.com

Facebook
Patricia Tard

www.ingramcontent.com/pod-product-compliance
Lightning Source LLC
Chambersburg PA
CBHW050705160426
43194CB00010B/2016